Reviews

"Michele has produced a drama that is born from a heart filled with love for St. Teresa of Avila. She captures the faith of the great saint whose story is fitting in this age of a profound renewal of the Church. She acts with a conviction inspired by Teresa."

Fr. James F. Kauffmann, SSL

"Ms. Morris in *Teresita* exceeded our expectations with the depth of the story, the poignancy of the message, and the sheer entertainment value. She puts a human face on this saint whose lofty reputation can have a dehumanizing effect. I highly recommend her show for audiences of children and adults alike. For us, one performance was not enough."

Fr. Robert Novokowsky, FSSP

"Michele Morris has created a compelling and important script and performs it with dynamic sincerity. Her one-woman play, *Teresita*, reaches out to us and penetrates into the depths of what each of us defines as 'faith.' I am so pleased to recommend that you experience this show!"

Larry Gard, Artistic Director,
Carpenter Science Theatre Company

TERESITA

A one-act play
based on the life of
St. Teresa of Avila

Michele Morris

LEONINE PUBLISHERS
PHOENIX, ARIZONA

Copyright © 2012, 2016, Michele A. Morris
Photograph of author, by Margaret Moriarty.

Caution: Professionals and amateurs are hereby notified that TERESITA, by Michele Morris, is subject to a royalty. It is fully protected under the copyright laws of the United States of America, the British Commonwealth, including Canada, and all other countries of the Copyright Union. All rights, including professional, amateur, motion picture, recitation, lecturing, public reading, radio broadcasting, television, and the rights of translation into foreign languages are strictly reserved.

In its present form, the play is dedicated to the reading public only. The amateur live stage performance rights to TERESITA are controlled exclusively by Leonine Publishers LLC, and royalty arrangements and licenses must be secured well in advance of presentation. Royalty of the required amount must be paid whether the play is presented for charity or gain and whether or not admission is charged.

When applying for a royalty quotation and license, please give the number of performances intended, dates of production, your seating capacity, and admission fee.

All rights reserved. No part of this work may be reproduced or transmitted in any form or by any means, electronic or mechanical, including photocopying, recording, or by any information storage or retrieval system now existing or to be invented, without written permission from the respective copyright holder(s), except for the inclusion of brief quotations in a review.

Published by Leonine Publishers LLC
Phoenix, Arizona, USA

ISBN-13: 978-1-942190-29-5

Printed in the United States of America

Visit us online at www.leoninepublishers.com
For more information: info@leoninepublishers.com

Thank you to Mom, Angela, and all
my family and friends throughout
Heaven and earth!

With a special thank you to
Larry Gard, Trisha Potter, and
Mater Ecclesiae Fund for Vocations

I dedicate this labour of love

~ to everyone who has ever wrestled with the
question: "What do You want of me?"

~ to my Carmelite family

~ to Fr. Robert Novokowsky

About the Play

Known as Teresita to her friends and family, nineteen-year-old Teresa de Cepeda y Ahumada asks for her father's permission to enter Carmel of the Incarnation. He refuses. In a passionate and decisive moment, Teresa leaves home in the middle of the night without her father's knowledge. Teresa reflects on her life's experiences that led her to this imminent decision.

Playwright's Notes

The question "What do You want of me?" comes directly from St. Teresa of Avila's poem: "In the Hands of God." This universal question resonates in the hearts of the faithful who strive to follow the will of God. This question moves our lives forward in surprising and unexpected ways. It is a constant question, demanding the exploration by restless hearts of endless possible answers. It is a question for courageous souls.

St. Teresa is one such brave and vivacious soul. Narrowing her life down into a manageable one-woman play was quite the challenge. I chose to focus on the dramatic moment of her decision to leave home: a decision made with pain and struggle. As the story unfolds, we discover not a lofty, untouchable saint, but a young everyday girl who is torn between the love she has for her family and the desire to follow God and to see what He wants of her.

The events in this play are factual. The reflections on the events in St. Teresa's life as expressed in the play are my own interpretation. Inspired by many of her own thoughts, combined with my friends' and my own experiences, I hope I have conveyed an honest and respectful portrait of this remarkable woman.

Michele Morris
March, 2015

Production Notes

Teresita was originally written as a touring production. Minimal set and properties allow for intimate performance spaces, although large venues work just as well. The set and blocking contained in this script are from the original production. Both can be adapted for various types of venues. Ideally, however, the set and blocking will be as simple as possible so the dynamic character of St. Teresa and her message remain the focus.

Setting

The play takes place in 1535 in Avila, Spain. The set is suggestive of Teresita's room in her father's house. Upstage Right is a chair and a small table (desk) in front, both facing full front. Downstage Left is another chair facing ¾ Stage Right and another small table directly behind it. The tables used for touring were wooden TV tray tables; the chairs also were wooden.

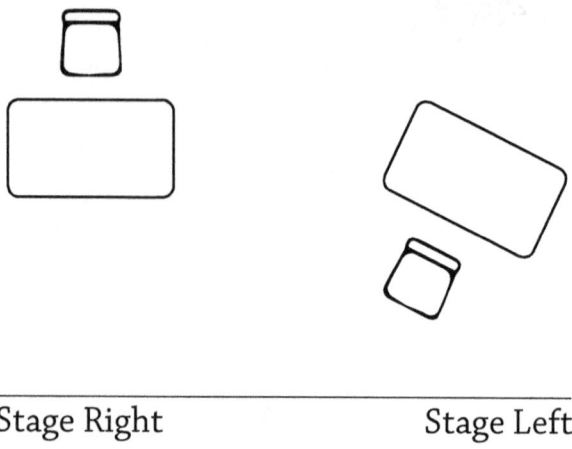

Stage Right   Stage Left

There is one entrance and exit. Its location is dependent upon the venue. The chairs and tables can be placed accordingly.

Properties for the Production

Props:

On Stage Right table:

1 hardcover book

1 satchel

1 Rosary

1 small prayer book

On Stage Left table:

1 hardcover book

1 triptych (or small statue) of the Blessed Virgin Mary

1 child's toy

Costume:

16th century Spanish gown complete with cap

Black or brown mantle (coat)

Lights:

Lights should also be simple; fading up at the beginning of the play and fading out at the end.

Sound:

Originally, there was no sound design. However, appropriate pre- and post-show music enhances the production.

Running Time: 45 minutes

The play debuted on July 16, 2013, the Feast of Our Lady of Mount Carmel, at St. Benedict Catholic Church, Richmond, Virginia, with the following cast and crew:

Teresita: Michele Morris

Directors: Stephanie Pyle and
              Michele Morris

Costume: Suzan McKenzie

Director's Notes

Accents

Accents can be tricky and distracting if the actress is not perfectly comfortable and accurate in her line delivery. For this production, the director and actress should not be concerned about using a Castilian accent. Rather, the focus should be on character development and the art of storytelling. However, the names of people mentioned in the play should be pronounced with the appropriate inflections. Below is a pronunciation guide:

ñ = *gn* as in lasagna
c before e or i = *th*

Cepeda	*pronounced*	The PAY da
Ahumada	*pronounced*	Au MA da
Briceño	*pronounced*	Bree THÁYN yo
Doña (a title)	*pronounced*	DON ya

Blocking

The script as presented here does not contain all the nuances of the original movements but hopefully provides a balance between helpful direction and freedom for creativity. Although the whole set reflects Teresita's room, the directors and actress of the original production designated the Stage Right area as the present moment and the Stage Left area for past moments (i.e.: when Teresita shares her memory of the convent of Our Lady of Grace).

Portraying Teresita

St. Teresa of Avila is an avid storyteller. Her spirited nature combined with her great love of people makes her an engaging personality. The actress portraying Teresita must capture the audience's heart, truly seeing them as dear friends and confidantes. The actress should revel in the stories Teresita shares and delight in the reactions of those whom she is addressing.

The script provides many transitional movements between speaking directly to the audience and internal reflection. Only a few are pointed out; the rest can be left up to the imaginations of the director and actress.

The best way to get to know St. Teresa is to read her autobiography.

You will never be the same.

TERESITA

TERESITA: (*Enters, distraught.*) What does he want of me? (*Stops. Looks back toward the door.*) What?! (*Paces about the room.*) He said no. Father said no. Not that I blame him. My behavior over the past few years hasn't shown him any signs of convent material, so it seems very sudden that I'm practically begging permission to become a nun. (*Stops. Looks at audience.*) He doubts my motivation. (*Shakes her head, sighs.*) I wonder, too, at my motivation for wanting such a strict and structured life. I imagine it has less to do with my devotion to God and more to do with... with what? (*Crosses to STAGE RIGHT chair, sits.*) My disdain for material possessions? The latest fashions, hair styles, make-up? Yes, at one time, these things did mean a great deal to me and here in Avila, distractions do come easily. I am not the same as I once was. Material possessions mean nothing to me. I have no attachments to them. But...people? (*TERESITA gazes at the audience and takes in each person, stifling her tears.*) My friends? My family? How will I let go of them? Especially my father.

(*Smiles. Stands.*) Alonso de Cepeda. My father. (*Moves DOWN STAGE.*) He is so dear to me and I to him. Of all my brothers and sisters, I am the closest to him, though the most troublesome. In his eyes I can do no wrong, which made deceiving him all-too-easy. My father is a good, good man, and very holy. His wealth does not interfere with his devotion to God. He loves life, but he loves prayer more. He dresses in the finest clothes and attends the finest parties, but he never lets those things rise above his prayer life. He is devoted to the Rosary. In fact, I don't think I've ever seen him leave the house without it. He may have great conversations with his peers about the state of the world and the earthly court, but at home he engages us in even greater discussions about the state of Heaven and the eternal court.

(*Savoring the words "eternity" and "forever."*) Ah, eternity! Forever! I have always been fascinated by that word. FOR-EV-ER. For*ever*. I could say that word over and over again, forever. (*Laughs.*) When I was a child, I did indeed repeat the word over and over again, much to the annoyance of my family. I couldn't help it! How can anyone understand "forever," let alone a child? Oh, I was obsessed with the word and what it truly meant. I still am. Our lives here on earth are limited. We will die *some*day. (*Smiles serenely.*) But, to live on forever, in Heaven! Well, naturally in Heaven. Who on earth would want to live forever in Hell? Certainly not me! And what is the best, the quickest, the most efficient way to live forever in Heaven? Become a martyr. (*Smiles, chuckles.*) Oh, the endless stories Mother and Father would share about the men and women who died for their faith! (*Crosses to STAGE LEFT chair.*) I would sit at my mother's feet as she colorfully described the events leading up to a particular martyr's death. I think my father felt she delved into a little too much detail, but I devoured every word. In my imagination, I transported myself out of Avila. No longer was I Teresa de Cepeda y Ahumada, but I was St. Lucy, St. Agnes, (*stands*) St. Columba of Córdoba! Oh, the adventures these women and men had! In my imagination, I faced everything they faced, including their untimely and unseemly deaths. (*Speaking as 7-year-old Teresita:*) "Mother, when they died, they went straight to Heaven, yes?" (*As Mother:*) "Yes, Teresita." (*As 7-year-old Teresita:*) "And they live in Heaven *fooo*orever, yes?" (*As Mother, exasperated:*) "Yes, Teresita." (*To Audience:*) And with that "yes," I determined that I, too, was going to become a martyr and live forever.

But, as I began to secretly plot my demise, I couldn't decide what kind of death I wanted. There were so many options! And none to my satisfaction. For instance, being burned at the stake or stoned to death would take too long; I wanted to live in Heaven forever, immediately—I needed a quick death! And just when I thought my martyrdom was never going to happen, I overheard Mother and Father speaking about recent events, which piqued my curiosity. (*Tiptoes toward STAGE LEFT chair and eavesdrops.*) They were speaking in hushed tones and sounded very distressed, which told me that what they were talking about was not for children's ears, so I leaned in closer and listened intently! Of course the only thing I understood out of the grown-up conversation was that the Moors were beheading Christians. (*Gasps!*) Beheading! THAT'S how I wanted to die! A quick death to my liking; I bet I wouldn't even feel the blade...if they remembered to sharpen it. Now, to formulate the plan.

(*Crosses to STAGE RIGHT table.*) Practically speaking, I knew I couldn't do this on my own. I *was* only seven years old. I would need a travel companion. Of all my siblings, I knew that my brother Rodrigo would take the least convincing. He's a few years older than I, but we were very close and I knew I could easily lure him into my escapade. (*Picking up satchel.*) So, we each packed a satchel, filling it with bread. Then early the next morning, just before dawn, we tiptoed outside. Now... (*Looking around; deciding.*) Where's Africa? (*Points in random direction with determination.*) That way! So we walked on. Rodrigo blindly followed my lead and although I wasn't sure if we were headed in the right direction, I was too determined and too proud to admit it.

(*As little Teresita to Rodrigo:*) "Come *on*, Rodrigo, *this* way! Yes! Come on, hurry. Come on!" (*On the last "Come on!" she turns and "sees" Uncle Pedro approaching.*) "Uh-oh."

(*To Audience:*) As it turned out we didn't get very far; our uncle happened to come riding up on horseback. He was on his way to our house but stopped when he recognized us. He questioned us with intense curiosity. Even though I had sworn Rodrigo to secrecy, he wilted under the concern gaze of our uncle. He spilt out our whole plan and then blamed me! Well, yes, I was to blame, but he didn't have to come right out and say so! (*Crosses STAGE RIGHT and places satchel back on table.*) Uncle Pedro escorted us back to our house. Mother and Father were relieved to have their children safely home with their heads still attached, and also happy, I'm sure, to have the mystery of the missing bread solved. For a brief moment I wondered which they missed more: their children or the bread! (*Slight pause, smiling at the memory.*) They sent us to our rooms to await punishment, but as I closed my door, I could hear them laughing. (*Mimicking her mother's voice:*) "Oh, that little Teresita! What ever shall we do with her?" Leave it to parents to upset the plans of their children! God, however, instilled in me a curiosity for Him, which I chose to ignore. Oh, my stubbornness! Battling with my conscience is tiresome. I don't know how to explain it. I felt, and still feel, torn between heeding a gentle invitation to be with God and remaining here with my family, my friends, and, yes, material wealth. (*Sits in STAGE RIGHT chair. Looks about her room.*) Do I stay here where all is familiar, comfortable, and safe? Or, do I take the risk and venture into the unknown? (*Stands.*) I am preparing to leave my home without my father's knowledge. I am going to sneak out in the middle of the night! Does this make me a coward? (*Moves STAGE RIGHT; paces.*) I've asked my father permission to enter Carmel. He said no. Honor thy father and thy mother. (*Stops pacing.*) But to whom do I answer—my father on earth or my Father in Heaven? I am unsure and fearful.

One fear that took me a long time to overcome was that I somehow caused my mother's death. I was twelve at the time and had never lost anyone so close to me. I confided in her. I sought her counsel. What did I say? What did I do to cause her death? Why did she leave me? I became sick with the realization of all that I had lost when she died and how much I had taken her for granted.

(*Pauses and smiles a little sadly, remembering her mother.*) Beatriz de Ahumada, my mother, is—was—a virtuous woman. She taught me the importance of prayer. She taught me the Rosary and shared with me all the stories about the saints and martyrs. She gave alms to the poor and encouraged me to do the same. She was grounded in her faith and no matter how rebellious I became, I could always count on her steadfast presence. She was my guide, my teacher, my light. Who now was going to be my example? Who could I turn to for spiritual guidance? My much older sister, Maria? (*Crosses to STAGE LEFT chair, sits.*) No. I was resistant to anything she had to say. We had nothing in common. While she grew in prudence in every way, I remained insolent. I couldn't relate to her. When Mother died, she took over the role of Mother. I wasn't ready or willing to come under her wing. To whom could I turn? Who would understand? No one. (*Pauses.*) No one…except… (*Stands and swiftly takes several steps DOWN CENTER. Kneels in prayer, pleading:*) Mary, O merciful Mary, my mother is gone and I am lost. You are my only mother now. You must guide and protect me. Oh, Mother Mary, please, what do I do? What do *you* want of me? (*Pauses, listening for a reply. None comes and she rises, exasperated.*)

There is nothing more disappointing than asking a direct question and receiving no response! (*Crosses to STAGE RIGHT chair, sits.*) Oh, I am confident that Mary heard my prayer. I just didn't feel her presence. Looking back now, I know she watched over me, protecting me from making choices that would dishonor my family. (*Glances at book on desk; picks it up.*) But, that isn't to say I didn't tempt danger.

(*Indicating book.*) A romance novel. My mother had a healthy fondness for them. I say healthy because, although these books contain unspeakable pleasures, my mother remained chaste. Her faith never wavered under these tantalizing and *scin*tillating stories. I, on the other hand, became profoundly influenced. (*Places book on desk, steps STAGE RIGHT, shakes her head and smiles sadly. Perks up at the following memory:*) I had long ago given up the idea of becoming a martyr. After my failed attempt at getting myself beheaded, I convinced Rodrigo that we should live as hermits. So we gathered stones in our yard and piled them up to make a hermitage. But, as the stones kept falling down, so, too, fell my desire to pursue anything religious. About that time, oh, a little while later, my mother beckoned me to her room—oooh, the intrigue! We were never allowed in our parents' room! (*Moving toward STAGE LEFT chair.*) But, she beckoned me in and closed the door. (*Picks up book on STAGE LEFT table and sits on STAGE LEFT chair.*) We sat on her bed; she opened up a book, began reading…and…oh, my! Romance! Chivalry! The women in these stories were quite different from the saints my mother first introduced me to. And the *men* with *whom* these women gave into temptation…oh, my. (*Stands, crosses CENTER.*) At first I was astounded that my mother read such books, but soon my astonishment gave way to obsession. I couldn't get enough of these books! No sooner did I finish one than I started another.

My father did not approve of my reading such material, so I made sure he was not around when I did. (*Slight pause, sadly:*) Thus began my sneaking around behind his back. I had never kept anything from my father, but once I started down that path it was so easy to do and so very difficult to stop. Had my mother not died in such a critical moment of my life between girlhood and womanhood—I never would have—(*Catches herself. Slams book shut, paces. To herself:*) No! It is so easy to accuse others for the messes we find ourselves in but if we are truly honest, we only have ourselves to blame. I am accountable for my own behavior and actions. I am responsible for the choices I make in my life: no one else. (*Almost slamming book on STAGE LEFT table.*) I felt so alone, so abandoned. (*Sits on STAGE*

LEFT chair. To audience:) Maria tried, my sister did try, but my stubbornness prevailed. I tolerated her. I placated her. (*Sighs.*) In the end I snuck behind her back as well.

(*Crosses to STAGE RIGHT table; picks up book.*) Despite Maria's disapproving glances, I delved deeper into the romance novels and...forget the company of Heaven, I wanted the company of men! (*Looks about the audience as she realizes the possible implications of her statement*) No! Oh no! No, no, no...not, *men*—but—people! Friends, family, and, yes, men included. I, after all, grew up in a house filled with men! My father and nine brothers. Yes, nine brothers. My father may have doted on me, but my brothers were relentless in the way brothers are. A young girl could not afford to be mousy living in a house filled with men. My courageous brothers ignited my own sense of adventure! I certainly was fascinated with men—they are an odd sort—but I never let my fascination in any way tarnish my father's reputation. I love and respect my father too much to do anything unsavory. Just the mere thought of doing something like that is repugnant! But, oh, to be engaged in laughter and good conversation with practically anybody. I *love* people, all kinds of people, (*Gives a mischievous smile*) and it is here, where I chose to keep company with my cousins who embodied the adventurous, romantic spirit I wished to emulate. My father, I know, did not approve of my spending so much time with them, (*Crosses back to STAGE RIGHT table; places book down*) but how could he stop me? They're family! (*Pause.*) The more time I spent with my cousins the more I cared about what others thought of me. Whenever I went out, I took the greatest care with my appearance: I wore lots of make-up and perfume; I adorned myself in all sorts of jewels and stones! Reading about romance and chivalry no longer satisfied me, I wanted to experience it!

Avila, the City of Knights, certainly had its fill of romantic and chivalrous moments! Yet, none could compare to the festivities which were about to unfold. (*Glancing in opposite direction, TERESITA sees her cousin, calls out and crosses to her:*) "Cousin! Cousin! What is going on? What news?" (*Eyes now wide with surprise and joy.*) "The Empress?! The Empress and her son are arriving here?!" (*To audience:*) The Empress chose Avila for her son's investiture ceremony! Oh, what a transformation! Banners and decorations adorned the town! Beautiful rich tapestries streamed from the windows! Games and tournaments! Music, song and dance permeated the streets! Excitement! Gossip! All the ingredients needed to entice an imaginative, adventurous, impressionable young lady seeking romance and chivalry! A four-month jubilant celebration— (*Changes her voice to reflect her father's calling her to attention.*) "Teresita." (*Ignoring her father, speaking to audience:*) A four-month jubilant celebration— (*In her father's voice:*) "Teresita!" (*To audience, resigned:*) which I was not to be a part of. (*Crosses to STAGE LEFT chair.*)

"Yes, Father? Our Lady of Grace? A boarder! But I—" (*Stops abruptly as if her father has silenced her.*)

(*Stunned.*) All I could do was nod. I had forgotten how to breathe. My father, my dearly beloved father, was sending me away! To a convent no less! I am his favorite. How could he do this to me? I have done nothing…nothing…except…flirt with danger. (*Sighs.*) Perhaps he has always been aware of my growing reckless behavior and chose for a time to turn a blind eye and believe only the good in me. (*Defeated, to herself:*) O wretched fool that I was!

(*Crosses STAGE LEFT and places herself at Our Lady of Grace. To audience:*) The Augustinian Sisters of Our Lady of Grace run a boarding house for young girls, educating them in all things, including spirituality. Oh, how miserable was I! Gone were my fine gowns and jewels; gone were festivities and living well. Here I learned to be poor. And the difference between being *poor* and being *poor in spirit*. I had never struggled so much with who I was or what was expected of me. What did *they* want of me? The other boarders were nice enough girls but they were not my family. The sisters seemed so austere. I felt remarkably out of place. (*Slight pause, enjoying the memory of Doña Maria.*) One nun befriended me, and I took an instant liking to her. Doña Maria de Briceno, our directress, was the nun in charge of boarders. She came from a Castilian aristocratic family so she could empathize with my struggles in transitioning from worldly affairs to spiritual ones. I met with her on a regular basis. (*Pauses slightly.*) As I poured out my troubled heart, I could feel my anger, resentment, and loneliness dissolving into a kind of emptiness. In that emptiness I discovered new understandings about myself and those around me. The other girls were not blood family, but we were in many other ways familial. We worked together and studied together. Together we ate and played and struggled. Our conversations had substance! The sisters, too, when they spoke, conveyed such depth. Yes, the sisters seemed austere, but their strict and structured lives gave them a sense of security and freedom I—I still cannot explain. I watched these simple women, who were not so simple. Despite their hardships and sufferings, their hearts and eyes shown with a joy I wanted for myself.

So, I spent as much time as I could with the sisters, engaging them in conversations, asking them about their lives. They were so warm and welcoming! They took me under their wings and soon I found myself once again the center of attention. (*Smiles.*) But, it was unlike anything I experienced. When I pranced about Avila, I received such flattering compliments. (*Mimicking various friends:*) "Oh, Teresita, you are breath-taking!" "Your hair is so lovely!" "How stunning you are in that gorgeous gown!" (*She shakes her head, dismayed.*) The more admiration I received, the more I craved it and the more I craved it, the more I sought it out. Living with the sisters, I recognize the deception of that kind of allurement, for it could never fill that longing, that desire for something more, something greater, than the shallowness in which I found myself.

But, the attention I receive from the sisters goes beyond the surface! They see me for *who* I am, not for *what* I am. They address me as Doña Teresa and not as "Teresita." They engage me on an intellectual level I have never experienced before. They have challenged me to live up to their high standards of physical, emotional, mental and spiritual living. I began to gain a true sense of self. (*Chuckles.*) Basically, I grew up. Something, though, was missing. I still did not have what they possessed...that inner joy. I brought this to the attention of Doña Maria who promptly responded: "Doña Teresa, perhaps you should pray more."

Pray more? Pray *more*?! That's all I've been doing since I've been here! Pray more. (*Shakes her head.*) What *kind* of prayer, though? Certainly I have been praying in community, chanting the Divine Office along with the other girls. Maybe the kind of prayer Doña Maria referred to is quiet prayer? (*Crosses to STAGE LEFT chair.*) So I began to pray quietly in my room. (*She sits at attention with eyes closed and folded hands. She yawns and nods off to sleep. Jerking awake she stands with arms out and again closes her eyes. She starts humming and swaying. With greater frustration, she kneels at STAGE LEFT chair, clasps her hands together, and bows her head. Sighing, she gives up. Still kneeling, but to audience:*) Being still and quiet is difficult to do when one is used to a more active life! (*Stands and sits in STAGE LEFT chair.*) However, with practice, I found myself in quiet prayer for longer periods of time. This enabled me to truly engage my inner thoughts and assess my emotions. In those moments, I recognized my misplaced attachments; I had been holding on so tightly to material possessions that I had lost my childhood faith. My desire for worldly pleasures had increased so much that any lingering thoughts I had of God had diminished. (*Stands.*) Ah! My father was not punishing me! He was protecting me! He knew long before I that the company I kept was leading me down the wrong path. He knew I needed a mother figure to guide me. (*Remembering her prayer to Mary.*) I did—I do. (*Crosses to STAGE LEFT table; picks up tryptic.*) Mother Mary. I had forgotten my pleas to her, but she never forgot mine. Mary protected me far more than I will ever know. And, my father? (*Puts image back on table.*) He did all he could but knew his efforts weren't enough. So he sent me to live under the guidance of the sisters, hoping I would discover what he already knew: The source of *true* joy is God. (*With new understanding, TERESITA crosses slowly CENTER STAGE. In awe.*) The sisters have God's joy! God's *joy* is what shines in their hearts and eyes! How do *I* reclaim God, the Joy of my youth? The God of "Forever"?!

(*The thought of becoming a nun enters her mind and at first reacts with revulsion. She pleads both with herself and with the audience. She gradually works up enough stress and heightened emotion that by "What do I want of me" she feels ill, which can be expressed through shortness of breath and coughing*).

Oh, no! No, no, no. No, I am *not* going to be a nun. I do not want to be a nun. I am not nun material! I want to be with my family. Do I want a family of my own? (*Considers the thought but is repelled by the idea.*) No, no. I don't want to be married! I *love* my family but I am *afraid* of marriage and all that it entails. But, I don't want to be a nun! I love God, but I'm *afraid* of eternity. I want to stay in this world, but I don't want to be a part of it. And, what of my friends? How do I tell them I want to be with them but do *not* want to return to my life prior to living with the sisters? What will they think? Will they understand? Will they cast me aside? No, no, no! It's not about what they think, or what they want! What do *I* want?! What do *I* want of me?!

(*Overcome with exhaustion, TERESITA sinks in STAGE RIGHT chair. Her voice changes to reflect weakness and illness, perhaps a hoarse, raspy whisper. Labored speech through "I still had not recovered," then voice gradually strengthens and returns to normal.*)

The sisters sent for my father, who brought me home to recover. I was sad to leave. I had come to embrace these spiritual women; I loved them. They had taught me so much about myself, about self-respect, about womanhood, about what is truly important in life; but I couldn't stay, not when I was so ill. After being home for a few days, I still had not recovered. My sister Maria sent word to Father, inviting me to stay with her and her family. (*Stands. Steps DOWN STAGE LEFT.*) So I went, and on my way, I stopped to visit Uncle Pedro. *He* is a holy man, much holier than even my father, if that is possible! His library teems with spiritual books and writings! The more I read these books and engaged in conversation with Uncle Pedro, the more conviction I had that the vanities of this world do indeed pass away, but the things of God live on forever!

(*Continues crossing STAGE LEFT.*) I continued on to my sister's house. What a wonderful reconciliation! We bonded like we never had before, sharing so many confidences. I cherish the intimacy that grew between us. (*Picks up child's toy from STAGE LEFT table.*) Our intimate moments, however, were often interrupted with the cries of her children. (*With awe.*) My sister, a mother! Although I was no longer tired from my illness, I was certainly tired from chasing little ones around the house. After two weeks with my sister's family, I became resolved in my conviction that married life is *not* for me. (*Places toy back on STAGE LEFT table.*) I certainly have gained greater appreciation for those who marry. The amount of work a woman performs all the days of her life deserves the utmost respect. I just could not see myself in the role of wife and mother. Something else was calling me, something greater than a family—*my* family.

(*Crosses to STAGE RIGHT chair and sits.*) I returned to my father's house determined to become a nun. But when I saw him, I melted and I couldn't ask him just then. I so enjoyed being with my father; we were closer than ever before. And, he was as happy to have me back home as he was glad to have someone take over the running of his household. I still had younger brothers and a sister who needed looking after! (*Pauses.*) I *was* happy to be with my family but—(*She pauses, conflicted.*) I was *not* happy to be home. (*Stands and crosses away from chair.*) I became tormented all over again about what to do with my life.

(*Determined.*) If I am going to do this—if I am going to become a nun—I am not entering Our Lady of Grace. As much I care for the sisters, I cannot see myself living such an arduous and rigorous way of life. But Carmel! Yes. The Convent of the Incarnation. They are less austere and my father can easily come and see me!

(*Rushes to STAGE LEFT chair, addressing her father:*) "Father! Father! I want to enter Carmel, and I need your permission!" (*Pauses.*) "No?! But why? This is what I want. I know this is what I'm supposed to do!" (*Incredulously turns away.*)

He said no. Father said no! (*Pauses, makes realization.*) He said no, *not now*. He asked me to wait until after he passes away. (*Crosses to STAGE RIGHT table. Packs satchel with prayer book and Rosary.*) I cannot wait that long! (*Pauses.*) Perhaps he does *not* doubt my motivations. He certainly was aware when I travelled down the wrong path; he must have been just as aware of my struggles in longing for God. Perhaps he truly believes my intentions for entering Carmel are genuine, but he doesn't want to lose *another* child to adventure. (*Moves CENTER—addresses audience:*) We are so close, so close, and I am torn. Honor thy father and thy mother. To whom do I answer? My father on earth or my Father in Heaven? I don't want to leave, but if I stay—if I don't leave now—I will never know what He wants of me: what God, my Father in Heaven, wants of me. (*Urgent look upward or at crucifix if there is one in the room, searching, demanding.*) What do You want of me?! (*Pauses, quietly pleads.*) *What?!* (*Pauses. Waits for an answer but doesn't seem to receive one. Turns slowly back to audience, resolved, introspective.*) There is only one way to find out. (*Crosses to STAGE RIGHT chair, takes mantle draped over chair and puts it on. She picks up satchel and heads for the door. In a bundle of mixed emotions, TERESITA stops, turns back to look around the room one last time. Exits.*)

Lights fade to black.

Blackout.

The End

In the Hands of God

I am Yours and born of You,
What do You want of me?
Majestic Sovereign,
Unending wisdom,
Kindness pleasing to my soul;
God sublime, one Being Good,
Behold this one so vile.
Singing of her love to You:
What do You want of me?

Yours, You made me,
Yours, You saved me,
Yours, You called me,
Yours, You awaited me,
Yours, I did not stray.
What do You want of me?

Good Lord, what do You want of me?
What is this wretch to do?
What work is this,
This sinful slave, to do?
Look at me, Sweet Love,
Sweet Love, look at me,
What do You want of me?

Teresita

In Your hand
I place my heart,
Body, life and soul,
Deep feelings and affections mine,
Spouse — Redeemer sweet,
Myself offered now to You,
What do You want of me?

Give me death, give me life,
Health or sickness,
Honor or shame,
War or swelling peace,
Weakness or full strength,
Yes, to these I say,
What do You want of me?

Give me wealth or want,
Happiness or gloominess,
Heaven or hell,
Sweet life, sun unveiled,
To You I give all.
What do You want of me?

Give me, if You will, prayer;
Or let me know dryness,
And abundance of devotion,
or if not, then barrenness.
In You alone, Sovereign Majesty,
I find my peace,
What do You want of me?

Give me then wisdom,
Or for love, ignorance,
Years of abundance,
or hunger and famine.
Darkness or sunlight,
Move me here or there:
What do You want of me?

If You want me to rest,
I desire it for love;
If to labor,
I will die working:
Sweet Love say
Where, how and when.
What do You want of me?

Calvary or Tabor give me,
Desert or fruitful land;
As Job in suffering
Or John at Your breast;
Barren or fruited vine,
Whatever be Your will:
What do You want of me?

Be I Joseph chained
Or as Egypt's governor,
David pained
Or exalted high,
Jonas drowned,
Or Jonas freed:
What do You want of me?

Teresita

Silent or speaking,
Fruitbearing or barren,
My wounds shown by the Law,
Rejoicing in the tender Gospel;
Sorrowing or exulting,
You alone live in me:
What do You want of me?

Yours I am, for You I was born:
Yours I am, for You I was born:

What do You want of me?

~ St. Teresa of Avila

 **About Leonine Publishers**

Leonine Publishers LLC makes fine Catholic literature available to Catholics throughout the English-speaking world. Leonine Publishers offers an innovative "hybrid" approach to book publication that helps authors as well as readers. Please visit our web site at www.leoninepublishers.com to learn more about us. Browse our online bookstore to find more solid Catholic titles to uplift, challenge, and inspire.

Our patron and namesake is Pope Leo XIII, a prudent, yet uncompromising pope during the stormy years at the close of the 19th century. Please join us as we ask his intercession for our family of readers and authors.

Do you have a book inside you? Visit our web site today. Leonine Publishers accepts manuscripts from Catholic authors like you. If your book is selected for publication, you will have an active part in the production process. This book is an example of our growing selection of literature for the busy Catholic reader of the 21st century.

www.leoninepublishers.com

www.ingramcontent.com/pod-product-compliance
Lightning Source LLC
Chambersburg PA
CBHW031438040426
42444CB00006B/875